THE GREAT BOOK OF ANIMAL KNOWLEDGE

GREAT WHITE SHARKS

Vicious Predators of the Great Oceans

Introduction

Great white sharks are the biggest, scariest, and one of the most dangerous predatory fishes ever. Despite there being many attacks on humans by great white sharks, they don't actually like the taste of humans. Being on top of the food chain, great white sharks maintain the balance of the oceans, preventing any species from overpopulating and keeping species healthy by eating their sick members.

What Great White Sharks Look Like

Photo by Elias Levy (flickr.com/elevy), as licensed under CC BY 2.0 Generic

Great White Sharks are torpedo shaped fishes. They have two big fins on their side, some smaller fins near their tail, and one fin arising out of their back. Great White Sharks are scary looking animals. Their ragged sharp teeth are something lots of people are scared of.

Size and Weight

Photo by Elias Levy (flickr.com/elevy), as licensed under CC BY 2.0 Generic

The great white shark is the largest fish that hunts other animals (killer whales are bigger but they are not fishes). They measure 15 ft to more than 20 ft (4.6 to 6 meters) long! Great white sharks weigh around 5,000 pounds (2,200 kg).

Teeth

Great white sharks have around 300 super sharp teeth. Their upper row is full of triangular teeth while their bottom row is full of pointed teeth. Each tooth is jagged on its edges, so they can cut big prey easier. Great white sharks also shed their old teeth and produce new teeth to replace it.

Skeleton

Great white sharks don't have bones! Instead, their skeleton is made up of cartilage, a strong and flexible tissue that is also found in human ears. Because sharks don't have bones, their weight is reduced and they can save more energy.

Speed

Sharks are fast swimmers. Their torpedo shape and lightweight skeleton helps them speed through the water. Great white sharks can swim at speeds up to 15 miles per hour (24 km/h), and they can do a short burst of up to 25 mph (40 km/h)! Their speed allows them to be able to jump high out of the water!

Where Great White Sharks Live

Photo by Elias Levy (flickr.com/elevy), as licensed under CC BY 2.0 Generic

Great white sharks can be found in cool waters all over the world. They are most often seen around Australia, South Africa, and Mexico. They can be found in the surface of oceans and also in depths almost 4,000 feet (1,200 meters) deep.

What Great Whites Eat

Great white sharks are carnivores; they only eat meat. Great white sharks prey upon seals, otters, fish, types of whales, sea birds, turtles, dolphins, and just about any animal in the ocean.

Hunting

Photo by Lwp Kommunikació (flickr.com/lwpkommunikacio), as licensed under CC BY 2,0 Generic

Great white sharks are ambush hunters. They usually surprise their prey from below. How the great whites hunt depends on which prey they are hunting. Sometimes they just charge straight into the animal and kill it. Other times, like when they hunt elephant seals, they bite the animal first and wait for it to weaken. When it's already weak they will eat it.

Senses

Photo by Elias Levy (flickr.com/elevy), as licensed under CC BY 2.0 Generic

Great white sharks have an extraordinary sense of smell. If there is one drop of blood mixed in with 10 billion drops of water, a great white can smell it! Great white sharks also have a good sense of hearing and seeing. They can hear even small vibrations in the water, and they can see well during nighttime. Great white sharks can also feel the movement of water caused by other animals swimming around.

Color

Great white sharks get their name from the underside of their body which is colored white. Their topside is colored grey. This coloring makes it harder for their prey to see them. Looking from below the sun makes it harder to see their white underside, and from above the deep dark ocean makes it harder to see their topside.

Groups

Although great white sharks can survive by themselves. They sometimes like to stay with other sharks. These groups are called schools or shoals. Great white sharks sometimes hunt together and share their kill.

Communication

Little is known about how great white sharks communicate with each other. They don't make sounds and sharks usually live alone so it's very hard to study how they communicate. Scientists believe that sharks communicate through body language.

Breeding

There is also little known about great white shark reproduction. After mating, male sharks have no part in bringing up the young great white sharks.

Baby Great White

The eggs of a great white shark hatch inside the mother's stomach! While inside the stomach, baby sharks eat the eggs that haven't hatched. Great white sharks usually give birth to 2-10 babies. Baby great white sharks are called pups. Pups usually measure 5 feet (1.5 m) long and weight around 70 pounds (32 kg).

Life of a Great White

After leaving their mother's stomach, the young great white sharks have to swim away as quickly as possible to avoid being eaten by their mother. Great white sharks reach maturity at around 15 years old. Scientists are not sure how long the lifespan of a great white shark is. Some think they live as long as 70 years!

Predators

Great white sharks are very dangerous predators, and they are rarely preyed upon by any other animal. However, there are some incidents where killer whales have killed great white sharks. Sometimes groups of dolphins can attack a great white shark.

Vulnerable

Great white sharks are no longer an endangered species; instead, they are now considered a vulnerable species. Scientists are not exactly sure how many great white sharks there are left, but great white shark populations are growing due to conservation efforts.

Other Types of Sharks

There are lots of different types of sharks. Some of these sharks are: Whale sharks (the biggest fish in the world), Hammerhead sharks (their heads look like hammers), Tiger sharks (dangerous sharks with the 2nd most attacks on humans), Goblin sharks (probably the strangest looking shark, rarely seen because they live in very deep waters), and Zebra sharks (small sharks that eat small animals).

Relatives

The closest relatives to sharks are rays. Both of their skeletons are made of cartilage instead of bones. Other less well known relatives of sharks are a group of fish called chimaeras. Chimaeras also have skeletons of cartilage instead of bones.

Shark Attacks

Great white sharks are thought to be man-eaters by a lot of people, but that is not exactly true. Studies show that sharks don't actually prefer to eat humans. Great white sharks sometimes just test bite something to see if they want to eat it. It's still very scary to be bitten by a shark but at least they don't really like the taste of humans! Most shark attacks in the world come from great white sharks.

Get the next book in this series!

BEAVERS: Carpenters of the Animal Kingdom

Log on to Facebook.com/GazelleCB for more info

Tip: Use the key-phrase "The Great Book of Animal Knowledge" when searching for books in this series.

For more information about our books, discounts and updates, please Like us on FaceBook!

Facebook.com/GazelleCB